ollins

INHERITANCE, VARIATION AND EVOLUTION

SNAP
REVISION

INFECTION AND RESPONSE & INHERITANCE, VARIATION AND EVOLUTION

AQA GCSE Biology

G000136467

AQA
GCSE
BIOLOGY

REVISE TRICKY
TOPICS IN A SNAP

Contents

Published by Collins
An imprint of HarperCollinsPublishers
1 London Bridge Street,
London, SE1 9GF

© HarperCollinsPublishers Limited 2016

9780008218096

First published 2016

10 9 8 7 6 5 4 3 2 1

All rights reserved. No part of this publication may be reproduced, stored in a retrieval system, or transmitted, in any form or by any means, electronic, mechanical, photocopying, recording or otherwise, without the prior permission of Collins.

British Library Cataloguing in Publication Data.

A CIP record of this book is available from the British Library.

Printed in United Kingdom by Martins the Printers

ACKNOWLEDGEMENTS

The author and publisher are grateful to the copyright holders for permission to use quoted materials and images.

p17 stockshoppe /Shutterstock.com; p39 Eric Isselee/ Shutterstock.com

Every effort has been made to trace copyright holders and obtain their permission for the use of copyright material. The author and publisher will gladly receive information enabling them to rectify any error or omission in subsequent editions. All facts are correct at time of going to press.

HT Higher Tier content

How To Use This Book

To get the most out of this revision guide, just work your way through the book in the order it is presented.

This is how it works:

Revise
Clear and concise revision notes help you get to grips with the topic

Revise
Key Points and Key Words explain the important information you need to know

Revise
A Quick Test at the end of every topic is a great way to check your understanding

Practise
Practice questions for each topic reinforce the revision content you have covered

Review
The Review section is a chance to revisit the topic to improve your recall in the exam

Pathogens and Disease

You must be able to:

- Describe the main types of disease-causing pathogen
- Describe the symptoms and method of spread of measles, HIV, salmonella and gonorrhoea
- Explain the role of the mosquito in the spread of malaria
- Describe the symptoms and method of spread of rose black spot in plants.

Pathogens and Disease

- **Pathogens** are microorganisms that cause infectious (communicable) diseases.
- Pathogens may infect plants or animals.
- They can be spread by:
  - direct contact
  - water or air
  - **vectors** (organisms that carry and pass on the pathogen without getting the disease).
- The spread of infectious diseases can be reduced by:
  - simple hygiene measures, e.g. washing hands and sneezing into a handkerchief
  - destroying vectors
  - isolating infected individuals, so they cannot pass the pathogen on
  - giving people at risk a vaccination (see page 7).

Viral Pathogens

- Viruses reproduce rapidly in body cells, causing damage to the cells.
- **Measles** is a disease caused by a virus:
  - The symptoms are fever and a red skin rash.
  - The measles virus is spread by breathing in droplets from sneezes and coughs.
  - Although most people recover well from measles, it can be fatal if there are complications, so most young children are vaccinated against measles.
- **HIV** (human immunodeficiency virus) causes AIDS:
  - It is spread by sexual contact or exchange of body fluids, e.g. it can be transmitted in blood when drug users share needles.
  - At first, HIV causes a flu-like illness.
  - If untreated, the virus enters the lymph nodes and attacks the body's immune cells.
  - Taking antiviral drugs can delay this happening.
  - Late stage HIV, or AIDS, is when the body's immune system is damaged and cannot fight off other infections or cancers.
- Viruses can also cause plant diseases, for example tobacco mosaic virus (see page 10).

The Virus that Causes Measles

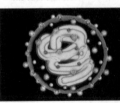

Key Point

It is not the HIV virus that directly kills people with AIDS. It is other infections, such as pneumonia, that a healthy body would usually be able to survive.

Bacterial Diseases

- Bacteria may damage cells directly or produce **toxins** (poisons) that damage tissues.
- **Salmonella** is a type of food poisoning caused by bacteria:
    - The bacteria are ingested in food, which may not have been cooked properly or may not have been prepared in hygienic conditions.
    - The bacteria secrete toxins, which cause fever, abdominal cramps, vomiting and diarrhoea.
    - Chicken and eggs can contain the bacteria, so chickens in the UK are vaccinated against salmonella to control the spread.
- **Gonorrhoea** is a sexually transmitted disease (STD) caused by bacteria:
    - It is spread by sexual contact.
    - The symptoms are a thick, yellow or green discharge from the vagina or penis and pain when urinating.
    - It used to be easily treated with penicillin, but many resistant strains have now appeared.
    - The use of a barrier method of contraception, e.g. a condom, can stop the bacteria being passed on.

The Bacteria that Cause Salmonella

Protists and Disease

Protists are single-celled organisms.
However, unlike bacteria, they are eukaryotic.
Malaria is caused by a protist:
- The protist uses a particular type of mosquito as a vector.
- It is passed on to a person when they are bitten by the mosquito.
- Malaria causes severe fever, which reoccurs and can be fatal.
- One of the main ways to stop the spread is to stop people being bitten, e.g. by killing the mosquitoes or using mosquito nets.

Mosquitoes Transmit Malaria

Fungal Diseases

Rose black spot is a fungal disease:
- It is spread when spores are carried from plant to plant by water or wind.
- Purple or black spots develop on leaves, which often turn yellow and drop early.
- The loss of leaves will stunt the growth of the plant because photosynthesis is reduced.
- It can be treated by using fungicides and removing and destroying the affected leaves.

> **Key Point**
>
> In malaria, the protist is the pathogen for the disease. The mosquito is acting as a parasite when it feeds on a person.

Quick Test

1. State one simple precaution that can stop pathogens being spread by droplets in the air.
2. Why is it important to keep uncooked meat separate from cooked meat?
3. Why does the contraceptive pill **not** prevent the spread of gonorrhoea?
4. Why should leaves infected with rose black spot be removed and burned?

> **Key Words**
>
> pathogen
> vector
> toxin

Human Defences Against Disease

You must be able to:

- Describe how the body tries to prevent pathogens from entering
- Describe how the immune system reacts if pathogens do enter the body
- Explain the process of immunity and how vaccinations work.

Preventing Entry of Pathogens

- The body has a number of non-specific defences against disease.
- These are defences that work against all pathogens, to try and stop them entering the body.

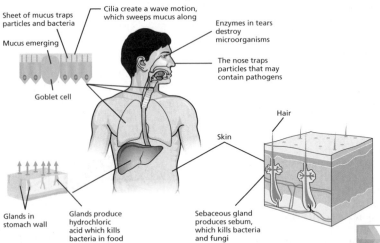

The Body's Defences

Sheet of mucus traps particles and bacteria

Cilia create a wave motion, which sweeps mucus along

Enzymes in tears destroy microorganisms

Mucus emerging

The nose traps particles that may contain pathogens

Goblet cell

Hair

Skin

Glands in stomach wall

Glands produce hydrochloric acid which kills bacteria in food

Sebaceous gland produces sebum, which kills bacteria and fungi

The Immune System

- If a pathogen enters the body, the immune system tries to destroy it.
- White blood cells help to defend against pathogens through:
  - phagocytosis, which involves the pathogen being surrounded, engulfed and digested

> **Key Point**
>
> Antibodies are specific to a particular pathogen, e.g. antibodies against gonorrhoea bacteria will not attach to salmonella bacteria.

White blood cell

Microorganisms invade the body.

The white blood cell finds the microorganisms and engulfs them.

The white blood cell ingests the microorganisms.

The microorganisms have been digested and destroyed.

- the production of special protein molecules called **antibodies**, which attach to **antigen** molecules on the pathogen

Antigens are markers on the surface of the microorganism.

The white blood cells become sensitised to the antigens and produce antibodies.

The antibodies then lock onto the antigens.

This causes the microorganisms to clump together, so that other white blood cells can digest them.

- the production of **antitoxins**, which are chemicals that neutralise the poisonous effects of the toxins.

Boosting Immunity

If the same pathogen re-enters the body, the white blood cells respond more quickly to produce the correct antibodies.
This quick response prevents the person from getting ill and is called **immunity**.
When a person has a **vaccination**, small quantities of dead or inactive forms of a pathogen are injected into the body.
Vaccination stimulates the white blood cells to produce antibodies and to develop immunity.

1 A weakened / dead strain of the microorganism is injected. Antigens on the modified microorganism's surface cause the white blood cells to produce specific antibodies.

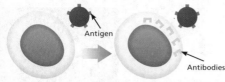

Antigen

Antibodies

2 The white blood cells that are capable of quickly producing the specific antibody remain in the bloodstream.

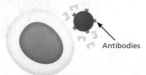

Antibodies

If a large proportion of the population can be made immune to a pathogen, then the pathogen cannot spread very easily.

Key Point

The disease smallpox does not exist anymore. This is because vaccination managed to prevent the pathogen spreading to new hosts. Scientists are hoping to repeat this with polio.

Key Point

Some vaccinations do carry a very small risk of side effects, but it is important to compare this with the risk of getting the disease.

Key Words

non-specific defences
immune system
phagocytosis
antibody
antigen
antitoxin
immunity
vaccination

Quick Test

1. How does the stomach help to kill pathogens?
2. What is phagocytosis?
3. What is the name of the protein molecules made by white blood cells when they detect a pathogen?
4. Why does vaccination use a dead or weakened pathogen?

Treating Diseases

You must be able to:

- Explain how antibiotics have saved lives and why their use is now under threat
- Describe how new drugs are developed
- HT Describe the production of monoclonal antibodies and explain why they are useful.

Antibiotics

- **Antibiotics**, e.g. penicillin, are medicines that kill bacteria inside the body. However, they cannot destroy viruses.
- Doctors will prescribe certain antibiotics for certain diseases.
- The use of antibiotics has greatly reduced deaths from infections.
- However, bacterial strains resistant to antibiotics are increasing (see page 23).
- **MRSA** is a strain of bacteria that is resistant to antibiotics.
- To reduce the rate at which resistant strains of bacteria develop:
  - doctors should **not** prescribe antibiotics:
    - unless they are really needed
    - for non-serious infections
    - for viral infections.
  - patients must complete their course of antibiotics so that all bacteria are killed and none survive to form resistant strains.

REQUIRED PRACTICAL	
Investigating the effect of different antibiotics on bacterial growth.	
Sample Method 1. Inoculate a Petri dish with a culture of bacteria. 2. Soak small discs of filter paper in different antibiotics. 3. Using forceps, place the antibiotic discs on the surface of the agar. 4. Incubate the sealed dish upside down at 25°C for several days.	**Considerations, Mistakes and Errors** • It is also possible to vary the concentration of the antibiotic to find the best concentration to use.
Variables • The independent variable is the type of antibiotic. • The dependent variable is the area around each disc that is clear of bacteria. The greater the area, the more effective the antibiotic is in killing the bacteria. • The control variables are the concentration of antibiotic used and the length of time that the discs are soaked.	**Hazards and Risks** • Care must be taken to follow aseptic techniques.

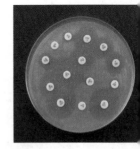

Developing New Drugs

- There is a constant demand to produce new drugs:
  - New painkillers are developed to treat the symptoms of disease but they do not kill the pathogens.
  - Antiviral drugs are needed that will kill viruses without also damaging the body's tissues.
  - New antibiotics are needed as resistant strains of bacteria develop.

Traditionally drugs were extracted from plants and microorganisms:
- **Digitalis** is a heart drug that originates from foxgloves.
- **Aspirin** is a pain killer that originates from willow.
- **Penicillin** was discovered by Alexander Fleming from the *Penicillium* mould.

Now most new drugs are synthesised (made) by chemists in the pharmaceutical industry. However, the starting point may still be a chemical extracted from a plant.
New medical drugs have to be tested and trialled before being used to make sure they are safe (not toxic).
If a drug is found to be safe, it is then tested on patients to:
- see if it works
- find out the optimum dose.

These tests on patients are usually **double-blind trials**:
- some patients are given a **placebo**, which does not contain the drug, and some patients are given the drug
- patients are allocated randomly to the two groups
- neither the doctors nor the patients know who has received a placebo and who has received the drug.

New painkillers are developed to treat the symptoms of disease – they do not kill pathogens
New antiviral drugs are needed that will kill viruses without damaging the body's tissues. This is not easy to achieve.

Monoclonal Antibodies

Monoclonal antibodies are produced from a single cell that has divided to make many cloned copies of itself.
These antibodies bind to only one type of antigen, so they can be used to target a specific chemical or specific cells in the body.
They are produced by combining mouse cells and a tumour cell to make a cell called a **hybridoma**.
Monoclonal antibodies can be used in different ways:
- in pregnancy tests, to bind to the hormone **HCG** found in urine during early pregnancy
- in laboratories, to measure the levels of hormones and other chemicals in blood, or to detect pathogens
- in research, to locate or identify specific molecules in a cell or tissue by binding to them with a fluorescent dye
- to treat some diseases, e.g. in cancer they can be used to deliver a radioactive substance, a toxic drug, or a chemical that stops cells dividing, specifically to the cancer cells.

Unfortunately, monoclonal antibodies have created more side effects than expected, so they are not yet widely used.

Quick Test

1. Why can antibiotics not be used to destroy HIV?
2. What term describes bacterial pathogens that are not affected by antibiotics?
3. Why did people once chew willow bark if they had a headache?
4. Why does the title 'double-blind trial' include the word 'double'?

> ## Key Point
>
> The purpose of a double-blind test is to ensure that it is completely fair. If the patients or doctors knew whether it was the drug or a placebo being used, it might influence the outcome of the test.

HT Monoclonal Antibodies

Vaccinate mouse to stimulate the production of antibodies

Collect spleen cells that form antibodies from mouse

Tumour cells (myeloma)

Spleen and myeloma cells fuse to form hybridoma cells

Grow hybridoma cells in tissue culture and select antibody-forming cells

Collect monoclonal antibodies

Key Words

antibiotics
MRSA
digitalis
aspirin
penicillin
double-blind trial
placebo
HT monoclonal antibody
HT hybridoma
HT HCG

Plant Disease

You must be able to:

- **HT** Describe how plant diseases can be detected and identified
- Describe the cause and symptoms of certain plant diseases
- Describe various methods that plants use to defend themselves from disease.

HT Detecting and Identifying Plant Disease

- There are a number of signs that a plant may be diseased:
  - stunted growth
  - spots on leaves
  - areas of decay (rot)
  - growths
  - malformed (abnormal) stems or leaves
  - discolouration
  - the presence of pests.
- To identify the disease, a number of steps can be taken:
  - consulting a gardening manual or website
  - taking infected plants to a laboratory to identify the pathogen
  - using testing kits, which contain monoclonal antibodies.

Examples of Plant Diseases

- Like animals, plants can suffer from non-communicable and communicable diseases.
- Plants can be infected by a range of viral, bacterial and fungal pathogens as well as by insects.
- Tobacco mosaic virus (TMV) is a widespread plant pathogen:
  - It infects tobacco plants and many other plants, including tomatoes.

- It produces a distinctive 'mosaic' pattern of discolouration on the leaves, which reduces chlorophyll content and affects photosynthesis.
- It affects the growth of the plant due to lack of photosynthesis.

Rose black spot is a fungal disease (see page 5).

Aphids are small insects often known as greenfly or blackfly. They feed from the phloem, taking sugars away from the plant.

Non-communicable diseases include a range of deficiency diseases, caused by a lack of mineral ions in the soil:
- Stunted growth is caused by nitrate deficiency, because nitrates are needed for protein synthesis.
- Chlorosis is caused by magnesium deficiency, because magnesium ions are needed to make chlorophyll.

Plant Defences

Plants have a number of physical defences to try and stop organisms entering them:
- cellulose cell walls
- a tough waxy cuticle on leaves
- layers of dead cells around stems (bark on trees), which fall off and take pathogens with them.

Some plants also have chemical defences, such as:
- antibacterial chemicals, which are made by plants such as mint and witch hazel
- poisons to deter herbivores, which are made by plants such as tobacco, foxgloves and deadly nightshade.

Other plants have evolved with mechanical adaptations, including:
- thorns and hairs to deter animals from eating or touching them
- leaves that droop or curl when touched
- mimicry to trick animals into not eating them or not laying eggs on the leaves, e.g. the white deadnettle does not sting, but it looks very similar to a stinging nettle.

Mimosa Leaves Curl Up to Deter Insects from Eating Them

White Deadnettle

Revise

Key Point

Aphids have long needle-like mouthparts, which they can insert straight into the phloem tubes of the plant.

Quick Test

1. Explain why the change in leaf colour caused by TMV can reduce photosynthesis.
2. What do aphids feed on?
3. Why does a lack of nitrates in the soil cause stunted growth?

Key Words

tobacco-mosaic virus (TMV)
aphid
deficiency disease
chlorosis
mimicry

Practice Questions

Pathogens and Disease

1. Draw **one** line from each type of pathogen to the disease that it causes.

bacterium		rose black spot
virus		malaria
protist		salmonella
fungus		measles

[3]

Total Marks _____ / 3

Human Defences Against Disease

1. Children are vaccinated against a range of diseases.
   Complete the sentences about vaccination.

   Vaccines contain _____ or _____ pathogens.

   These stimulate the white blood cells to produce _____ .

   This results in the children becoming _____ to the disease. [4]

2. The MMR vaccine was introduced in the UK in 1995.
   It protects children from three diseases: measles, mumps and rubella.

   a) What are the usual symptoms of measles? [2]

   b) Why is it important to vaccinate against measles? [1]

   c) The graph in **Figure 1** shows the uptake of the MMR vaccine in the UK between 1995 and 2007.

      i) What percentage of 2-year-olds was vaccinated in 2007? [1]

      ii) In which **two** years was there a significant decline in the uptake of the vaccine compared with the previous year? [2]

      iii) Suggest a reason for this decline. [1]

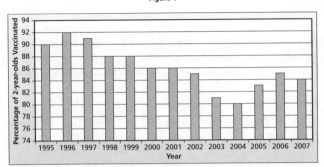

Figure 1

3 This is an extract from a leaflet about keeping healthy when travelling abroad.

> **In tropical areas, use an insect repellent.**
> **Check that you have been vaccinated against the diseases that you might come into**
> **contact with on your travels.**

a) Explain how using an insect repellent may help travellers to stay healthy. [3]

b) Explain why a person should be vaccinated before they go on holiday rather than
   waiting to see if they get the disease before getting vaccinated. [3]

4 People have different opinions about vaccinations.

Some say it is better to give children a combined vaccination, i.e. one injection containing
several vaccines.

Others say that children should have several injections each containing a single vaccine.

Four people were asked their opinions on the subject.

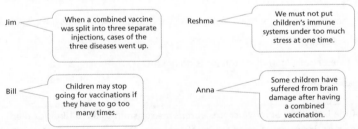

Which **two** people think that **combined** vaccinations are a **good** idea? [2]

Total Marks _____ / 19

Practice Questions

Treating Diseases

1 A student investigates the effect of different cleaning products on the growth of bacteria.
She sets up five agar plates that are seeded with one type of bacteria.
On each plate, she places four discs of absorbent paper, which have been soaked in a particular cleaning product.
The plates are incubated at 25°C for three days.
The student then measures the diameter of the area around the discs where bacteria have not grown.

Table 1 shows the results.

Table 1

Plate and Cleaning Product	Diameter of Area Around Disc Where Bacteria Did Not Grow (mm)				
	Disc 1	Disc 2	Disc 3	Disc 4	Mean
Plate 1 (soap)	1	2	2	1	1.5
Plate 2 (hand wash)	3	2	2	4	2.8
Plate 3 (kitchen cleaner)	5	4	6	5	5.0
Plate 4 (bathroom cleaner)	5	5	6	7	
Plate 5 (no cleaner)	0	0	0	0	0.0

a) Calculate the mean diameter of the area where bacteria did not grow for **Plate 4**. [2
Give your answer to one decimal place.

b) Which product was the most effective at killing the bacteria? [1

c) Why did the student use no cleaning product on **Plate 5**? [1

d) What has the student done to make her results reliable? [1

2 *Staphylococcus aureus* is a bacterium commonly found on human skin.
It can sometimes cause skin infections.
Most strains of this bacterium are sensitive to antibiotics and so these infections are easily cured.

a) i) What is an antibiotic? [2

ii) Name one type of pathogen that antibiotics do not affect. [1

b) A local newspaper reported that:

Some strains of the bacterium *Staphylococcus aureus* are resistant to an antibiotic called methicillin. They may also be resistant to many other commonly prescribed antibiotics. This is called multiple resistance.

It is difficult to get rid of these 'superbugs' when patients are infected with them.

To try and reduce the risk of 'superbugs' appearing, we have to take care when using antibiotics.

i) What is the abbreviation used for multiple resistant strains of *Staphylococcus aureus* that are resistant to many antibiotics including methicillin? [1]

ii) List the precautions that are being taken with antibiotics to try and stop resistant strains developing. [3]

3 New drugs undergo testing before they are made available to the public.

a) The statements below describe the main stages in drug development and testing. They are in the wrong order.

Number the stages **1** to **5** to show the correct order. Stage 1 has been done for you.

The drug is passed for use on the general public.	
Trials using low doses of the drug take place on a small number of healthy volunteers.	
A new drug is made in the laboratory.	1
Clinical trials take place involving large numbers of patients and volunteers.	
The drug is tested in the laboratory using tissue culture.	

[3]

b) Suggest **two** reasons why it is necessary for new drugs to undergo such testing. [2]

c) In clinical trials, one group of patients is often given a placebo.

i) What is a placebo? [1]

ii) Explain why a placebo is given. [2]

> Total Marks _____ / 20

Plant Disease

1 **Figure 1** shows an aphid feeding on a plant stem.

a) The aphid has mouthparts that allow it to feed from a tissue inside the stem.

Figure 1

Give the name of this tissue. [1]

b) Explain why many aphids feeding on a plant could stunt the growth of the plant. [2]

c) Explain how aphids could transmit pathogens from one plant to another. [2]

d) Before chemical pesticides became available, gardeners used to spray their plants with a solution made from tobacco plants.

Explain why they did this. [2]

> Total Marks _____ / 7

Sexual and Asexual Reproduction

You must be able to:

- Describe some examples of asexual reproduction in different organisms
- Explain why sexual reproduction involves meiosis
- Explain why organisms may reproduce sexually or asexually at different times.

Asexual Reproduction

- **Asexual reproduction** involves:
  - only one parent
  - no fusion of **gametes**, so no mixing of genetic information
  - the production of genetically identical offspring (clones)
  - mitosis.
- Many plants reproduce asexually and in different ways, e.g.
  - strawberry plants send out long shoots called **runners**, which touch the ground and grow a new plant
  - daffodils produce lots of smaller bulbs, which can grow into new plants.

> **Key Point**
>
> Gardeners use asexual reproduction to produce large numbers of identical plants (see page 25).

Daffodils

Bulb

Strawberry Plant

Runner

- Many fungi reproduce asexually by spores.
- Malarial protists reproduce asexually when they are in the human host.

Sexual Reproduction and Meiosis

- Sexual reproduction involves the fusion (joining) of male and female gametes:
  - sperm and egg cells in animals
  - pollen and egg cells in flowering plants.
- This leads to a mix of genetic information, which produces variation in the offspring.
- The formation of gametes involves **meiosis**.

Meiosis

Cell with two pairs of chromosomes (diploid cell).	Each chromosome replicates itself.	Chromosomes part company and move to opposite poles.	Cell divides for the first time.	Copies now separate and the second cell division takes place.	Four haploid cells (gametes), each with half the number of chromosomes of the parent cell.

When a cell divides by meiosis:
- copies of the genetic information are made
- the cell divides twice to form four gametes, each with a single set of chromosomes
- all gametes are genetically different from each other.

Meiosis is important because it halves the number of chromosomes in gametes.

This means that fertilisation can restore the full number of chromosomes.

Once fertilised, the resulting cell divides rapidly by mitosis and cells become specialised by differentiation.

Sperm		Egg		Fertilised Egg Cell
23 chromosomes	+	23 chromosomes	=	46 chromosomes (23 pairs) – half from mother (egg) and half from father (sperm)

Asexual Versus Sexual Reproduction

The advantages of sexual reproduction are:
- it produces variation in the offspring
- if the environment changes, any variation means that at least some organisms will be suited and can survive
- it allows humans to selectively breed plants and animals, and increase food production (see page 24).

The advantages of asexual reproduction are:
- only one parent is needed
- it is more time and energy efficient, as the organism does not need to find a mate
- it is faster than sexual reproduction
- many identical offspring can be produced to make the best use of good conditions.

Some organisms can reproduce both sexually and asexually:
- many plants can produce seeds by sexual reproduction and can also reproduce asexually, e.g. using bulbs and runners
- many fungi can make spores by asexual or by sexual reproduction
- malaria parasites reproduce sexually in the mosquito as well as asexually in humans.

Key Point

If organisms have a choice, they often reproduce asexually when conditions are good to make lots of well-suited offspring. Sexual reproduction is used when conditions are getting worse, e.g. there is a drop in temperature or lack of food.

Quick Test

1. What are strawberry runners?
2. How many gametes are made when one cell divides by meiosis?
3. The body cells of chickens have 78 chromosomes. How many chromosomes are in each gamete?
4. Which type of reproduction produces most variation?

Key Words

asexual reproduction
gamete
runners
meiosis

DNA and Protein Synthesis

You must be able to:

- Describe how the genetic material is arranged in a cell
- Describe the structure of DNA
- **HT** Explain how DNA can code for proteins and how this can go wrong.

The Genome

- The genetic material in the nucleus of a cell is made of a chemical called DNA.
- The DNA is contained in structures called chromosomes.
- A gene is a small section of DNA on a chromosome.

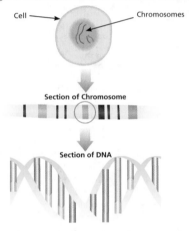

Cell — Chromosomes

Section of Chromosome

Section of DNA

Key Point

A person now has the choice to have their genome tested to see how likely it is that they may get certain disorders. This may be a difficult decision to take.

- Each gene codes for a particular sequence of amino acids, to make a specific protein.
- The genome of an organism is its entire genetic material.
- The whole human genome has now been studied and this may have some important uses in the future, e.g.
  - doctors can search for genes linked to different types of disorder
  - it can help scientists to understand the cause of inherited disorders and how to treat them
  - scientists can investigate how humans may have changed over time, and even how ancient populations may have migrated across the globe.

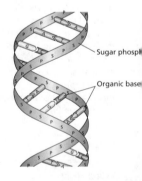

Sugar phosph

Organic base

The Structure of DNA

- DNA is a polymer made up of repeating units called nucleotides.
- Each nucleotide consists of:
  - a sugar
  - a phosphate
  - one of four bases: A, C, G or T.

A Single Nucleotide

Phosphate

Sugar

Organic ba

- The nucleotides are joined together to form long strands.
- Each molecule has two alternating sugar and phosphate strands, which are twisted to form a double helix.
  Attached to each sugar is one of the four bases.

HT It is an attraction between the different bases that holds the two strands together:
  - a C on one strand always links with a G on the opposite strand
  - a T on one strand always links with an A on the opposite strand.

The order of bases in a section of DNA...

Making Proteins

The order of bases on DNA controls the order in which amino acids are joined together to make a particular protein.
A sequence of three bases is the code for one amino acid.

...controls the order in which amino acids...

HT Proteins are synthesised on ribosomes using a template that has been taken from the DNA and carried out of the nucleus.
HT Carrier molecules then bring specific amino acids to add to the growing protein chain in the correct order.
HT When the protein chain is finished, it folds up to form a unique shape.
HT This unique shape allows the proteins to do their job as enzymes, hormones or structural proteins such as collagen.

...are joined together to form a protein.

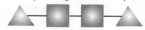

HT Mutations

A change in DNA structure is called a mutation.
If any bases in the DNA are changed, then it may change the order of amino acids in the protein coded for by the gene.
Mutations occur all the time. Most do not alter the protein, or only alter it slightly, so that it still works.
A few mutations may cause the protein to have a different shape:
  - If it is an enzyme, then the substrate may no longer fit into the active site.
  - If it is a structural protein, it may lose its strength.
Not all parts of DNA code for proteins:
  - Non-coding parts of DNA can switch genes on / off so that they can / cannot make specific proteins.
  - Mutations in these areas of DNA may affect how genes are expressed.

 Key Point

Certain chemicals and high-energy radiation can increase the rate at which mutations occur.

 Key Point

Very occasionally, a mutation may occur that is useful. Without this type of variation, evolution by natural selection would not occur (see page 22).

Key Words

DNA
chromosomes
gene
genome
polymer
nucleotide
HT collagen
HT mutation

Quick Test

1. What are chromosomes made from?
2. What is a section of chromosome called?
3. Name the three types of molecule that make up DNA.
4. HT What is a mutation?
5. HT Give a function of non-coding sections of DNA.

Patterns of Inheritance

You must be able to:

- Describe the contribution made by Gregor Mendel to the study of genetics
- Explain how ideas about genetics have changed since his work
- Predict the outcome of genetic crosses using genetic diagrams
- Describe examples of human genetic disorders
- Explain how sex is determined in humans.

Gregor Mendel

- Until the mid-19th century, most people thought that sexual reproduction produced a blend of characteristics, e.g. if a red flowering plant was crossed with a white flowering plant, then pink flowering plants were produced.
- Gregor Mendel investigated this by carrying out breeding experiments on pea plants.
- He found that characteristics are determined by 'units' that are inherited (passed on) and do **not** blend together.
- Later in the 19th century, the behaviour of chromosomes during cell division was observed.
- Then in the early 20th century, scientists realised that chromosomes and Mendel's 'units' behaved in similar ways.
- They decided that the 'units', now called genes, were located on chromosomes.
- In the mid-20th century, scientists worked out what the structure of DNA looked like and the mechanism by which genes work.
- The importance of Mendel's discovery was not recognised during his lifetime because:
    - he was a monk working in a monastery, not a scientist at a university
    - he did not publish his work in a well-known book or journal.

> ### Key Point
> The development of the gene theory, explaining how characteristics are passed on, is a good example of how ideas gradually change and develop. It illustrates how scientists make new observations and discoveries over time.

Modern Ideas About Genetics

- Some characteristics are controlled by a single gene, e.g. fur colour in mice and red-green colour blindness in humans.
- Each gene may have different forms called **alleles**, e.g. the gene for the attachment of earlobes has two alleles – attached or free.
- An individual always has two alleles for each gene:
    - One allele comes from the mother.
    - One allele comes from the father.
- The combination of alleles present in a gene is called the **genotype**, e.g. bb.
- How the alleles are expressed (what characteristic appears) is called the **phenotype**, e.g. blue eyes.
- Alleles can either be **dominant** or **recessive**.
- If the two alleles present are the same, the person is **homozygous** for that gene, e.g. BB or bb.
- If the alleles are different, they are **heterozygous**, e.g. Bb.

> ### Key Point
> A dominant allele is always expressed, even if only one copy is present. A recessive allele is only expressed if two copies are present, i.e. no dominant allele is present.

Genetic Crosses

- Most characteristics are controlled by several genes working together.
- If only one gene is involved, it is called **monohybrid inheritance**.
- Genetic diagrams or **Punnett squares** can be used to predict the outcome of a monohybrid cross.
- These diagrams use: capital letters for dominant alleles and lower case letters for recessive alleles.
- For example, for earlobes:
  - the allele for a free lobe is dominant, so **E** can be used
  - the allele for an unattached lobe is recessive, so **e** can be used.
- These Punnett squares show the possible outcomes of three crosses:

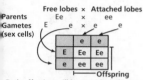

Each offspring will have a 1 in 2 chance of having attached lobes (because the dominant allele is present in half the crosses).

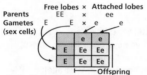

Each offspring will have free lobes (because the dominant allele is present in each cross).

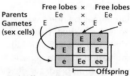

Each offspring has a 3 in 4 chance of having free lobes (because the dominant allele is present in three out of four crosses).

Genetic Disorders

- Some human disorders are inherited and are caused by the inheritance of certain alleles:
  - **Polydactyly** (having extra fingers or toes) is caused by a dominant allele.
  - **Cystic fibrosis** (a disorder of cell membranes) is caused by a recessive allele.

Sex Determination

- Only one pair out of the 23 pairs of chromosomes in the human body carries the genes that determine sex.
- These are called the **sex chromosomes**.
- In females, the two sex chromosomes are identical and are called X chromosomes (XX).
- Males inherit an X chromosome and a much shorter chromosome, called a Y chromosome (XY).
- As with all chromosomes, offspring inherit:
  - one sex chromosome from the mother (X)
  - one sex chromosome from the father (X or Y).

Quick Test

1. What are the different forms of a gene called?
2. What do we call a combination of one dominant and one recessive allele?
3. Does a recessive or dominant allele cause cystic fibrosis?
4. What sex chromosomes are present in a male liver cell?

Key Point

It is now possible to test unborn foetuses for a range of genetic disorders. However, this means that the parents may have to make difficult decisions about the future of their baby. There is also a small risk to the pregnancy when removing foetal cells to test.

Key Words

allele
genotype
phenotype
dominant
recessive
homozygous
heterozygous
monohybrid inheritance
Punnett square
polydactyly
cystic fibrosis
sex chromosomes

Variation and Evolution

You must be able to:

- Describe the main sources of variation between individuals
- Explain Darwin's theory of natural selection
- Describe some of the evidence for evolution.

Variation

- In a population, differences in the characteristics of individuals are called variation.
- This variation may be due to differences in:
  - the genes individuals have inherited (genetics)
  - the conditions in which individuals have developed (environment)
  - a combination of both genetic and environmental causes.
- Sexual reproduction produces different combinations of alleles and, therefore, variation, but only mutations create new alleles.
- Whereas most mutations do not affect the phenotype, a small number do. Within these, very rarely, a mutation may produce a phenotype that gives an organism a great survival advantage.

Natural Selection

- Evolution is the gradual change in the inherited characteristics of a population over time. This may lead to the formation of a new species.
- Many people have put forward theories to explain evolution.
- The theory that most scientists support is called natural selection, which was put forward by Charles Darwin.
- It states that all species have evolved from simple life forms that first developed more than three billion years ago.
- During a round-the-world expedition, Darwin observed:
  - Organisms often produce large numbers of offspring.
  - Populations usually stay about the same size.
  - Organisms are all slightly different – they show variation.
  - Characteristics can be inherited.
- Darwin used his observations to make these conclusions:
  - There is a struggle for existence.
  - More organisms are born than can survive.
  - The ones that survive and breed are the ones best-suited to the environment.
  - They pass on their characteristics to their offspring.
  - Over long periods of time the characteristics of populations change.
- In 1858, Alfred Russel Wallace suggested a similar theory to Darwin and this made Darwin realise that he should publish his ideas.
- Darwin published his theory in a book called *On the Origin of Species* in 1859.
- There was a lot of controversy over Darwin's ideas and several reasons why it took a long time for people to accept his theory:
  - The theory challenged the idea that God made all the organisms that live on Earth.

Key Point

ABO blood groups are controlled by a single gene, but height is the result of a combination of genes and environment. That is why there is a wide spread of possible heights.

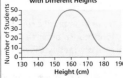

The Number of Students in My Year with Different Heights

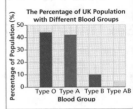

The Percentage of UK Population with Different Blood Groups

- There was not enough evidence at the time the theory was published to convince many scientists.
- The mechanism of inheritance and variation was not known until 50 years after the theory was published.
- There were other theories, including that of Jean-Baptiste Lamarck. Lamarck's theory was based on the idea that changes that occur in an organism during its lifetime can be inherited.
- We now know that, in most cases, this type of inheritance cannot occur.

Evidence for Evolution

- One problem with Darwin's theory has now been solved – we now know the mechanism of inheritance and variation, i.e. that characteristics are passed on to offspring in genes.
- There is also some evidence for evolution provided by fossils.
- Fossils are the remains of organisms from hundreds of thousands of years ago that are found in rocks.
- Fossils may be formed in various ways:
  - from the hard parts of animals that do not decay easily
  - from parts of organisms that have not decayed, because one or more of the conditions needed for decay was absent
  - when parts of the organisms are replaced by other materials as they decay
  - as preserved traces of organisms, e.g. footprints, burrows and root pathways.
- Scientists have used fossils to look at how organisms have gradually changed over long periods of time.
- Although fossils have been useful to scientists there are problems. There are gaps in the fossil record, because:
  - Many early forms of life were soft-bodied, which means that they have left very few traces behind.
  - What traces there were may have been destroyed by geological activity.
- The development of antibiotic-resistant strains of bacteria can be explained using the theory of natural selection:
  - Bacteria can evolve rapidly because they reproduce at a fast rate.
  - When they reproduce, mutations occur.
  - Some mutated bacteria might be resistant to antibiotics and are not killed.
  - These bacteria survive and reproduce, so a resistant strain develops (see page 8).
- There is still much debate today among scientists over the theory of evolution and the origins of life.

Lamarck believed that the necks of giraffes stretched during their lifetime to reach food in trees. They then passed this characteristic on to the next generation.

Darwin believed giraffes that had longer necks could reach more food in trees, so they were more likely to survive and reproduce.

Key Point

When scientists describe natural selection now, they can talk about alleles being passed on, which will cause changes to the phenotypes in a population.

Quick Test

1. Who developed the theory of evolution by natural selection?
2. Give **one** reason why the theory of evolution by natural selection was not accepted by Darwin's peers straight away.
3. Who described a theory of evolution where changes during the lifetime of an organism were passed on to the next generation?
4. Give **one** reason why there are gaps in the fossil record.

Key Words

variation
evolution
natural selection
fossils

Manipulating Genes

You must be able to:

- Describe the process of selective breeding
- Explain how genetic engineering can be used to change organisms' characteristics
- Compare different cloning techniques.

Selective Breeding

- Humans have been using selective breeding, or artificial selection, for thousands of years to produce:
  - food crops from wild plants
  - domesticated animals from wild animals.
- It is the process by which humans breed plants and animals with particular, desirable genetic characteristics.
- Selective breeding involves several steps:
  1. Choose parents that best show the desired characteristic.
  2. Breed them together.
  3. From the offspring, again choose those with the desired characteristic and breed.
  4. Continue over many generations.
- The type of characteristic that could be selected includes:
  - disease resistance in food crops
  - animals that produce more meat or milk
  - domestic dogs with a gentle nature
  - large or unusual flowers.
- However, selective breeding can lead to 'inbreeding', where some breeds are particularly prone to disease or inherited defects.

Genetic Engineering

- Genetic engineering is a more recent way of bringing about changes in organisms.
- It involves changing the characteristics of an organism by introducing a gene from another organism.

HT In genetic engineering:
  1. Enzymes are used to isolate the required gene.
  2. This gene is inserted into a vector, e.g. a bacterial plasmid or virus.
  3. The vector is used to insert the gene into the required cells.

HT If the genes are put into the cells of animals or plants at the egg or embryo stage, then all cells in the organism will get the new gene.

- Plant crops have been genetically engineered to:
  - be resistant to diseases, insects or herbicide attack
  - produce bigger, better fruits.
- Crops that have had their genes modified in this way are called genetically modified (GM) crops.

Example of Selective Breeding

Choose the spottiest two to breed...

... and then the spottiest of their offspring..

... to eventually get Dalmatians.

Key Point

Owners have to be very careful when mating pedigree dogs to make sure that they are not too closely related.

- Some people are concerned about GM crops and the possible long-term effects on populations of wild flowers and insects and on human health (if consumed).
- Other ethical considerations include the role that multinational companies play in manufacturing GM crops and setting the price.
- Fungi or bacterial cells have been genetically engineered to produce useful substances, e.g. human insulin to treat Type 1 diabetes.

Key Point

Genetic engineering is a good example of a new technology that could be very useful. However, there are ethical issues to consider.

Part of a human chromosome

Human insulin gene

Ring of bacterial DNA cut open

Human insulin gene inserted into bacterial DNA

- In the future, it may be possible to use genetic modification to cure or prevent some inherited diseases in humans.

Cloning

- Clones are genetically identical individuals.
- They are produced naturally by asexual reproduction (page 16).
- There are also a number of artificial ways of making clones.
- In plants, identical plants can be produced from:
  - cuttings – this is a method often used by gardeners
  - tissue culture – this uses small groups of cells to grow new plants and is used commercially and to preserve rare plant species.
- In animals, clones can be produced by splitting apart cells from an embryo before they become specialised, then transplanting the identical embryos into host mothers.
- It has also become possible to produce clones using adult cells:
  ❶ Remove the nucleus from an unfertilised egg cell.
  ❷ Insert the nucleus from an adult body cell of the organism you want to clone into the empty egg cell.
  ❸ Stimulate the egg cell to divide using an electric shock.
  ❹ Allow the resulting embryo to develop into a ball of cells.
  ❺ Insert the embryo into the womb of a surrogate female to continue its development.

1 Select a plant

2 Take cuttings

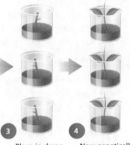

3 Place in damp atmosphere

4 New genetically identical plants develop

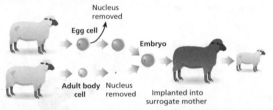

Nucleus removed

Egg cell

Embryo

Adult body cell

Nucleus removed

Implanted into surrogate mother

Key Words

selective breeding
genetic engineering
genetically modified (GM)
clone
cuttings
tissue culture
surrogate

Quick Test

1. State one characteristic that farmers might selectively breed cows for?
2. HT What is used to cut genes from chromosomes in genetic engineering?
3. Describe one concern about GM crops.
4. What is an electric shock used for in cloning?

Classification

You must be able to:

- Explain why classification systems have changed over time
- Describe why organisms may become extinct
- Explain how new species are formed
- Describe how evolutionary trees are constructed.

Principles of Classification

- Traditionally, living things have been classified into groups based on their structure and characteristics.
- One of the main systems used was developed by Carl Linnaeus.
- Linnaeus classified living things into:
  kingdom → phylum → class → order → family → genus → species
- Organisms are named by the binomial system, i.e. they have two parts to their Latin name:
  - The first part is their genus.
  - The second part is their species.
- New models of classification were proposed because:
  - microscopes improved, so scientists learnt more about cells
  - biochemical processes became better understood.
- Due to evidence, e.g. from genetic studies, there is now a three-domain system developed by Carl Woese.
- In this system organisms are divided into:
  - archaea (primitive bacteria, usually living in extreme environments)
  - bacteria (true bacteria)
  - eukaryota (including protists, fungi, plants and animals).

Key Point

The scientific name for lion is *Panthera leo* and for tiger it is *Panthera tigris*. This shows that they are in the same genus but different species. The cheetah is called *Acinonyx jubatus* – it is in a different genus and species.

Extinction

- Throughout the history of life on Earth, different organisms have been formed by evolution and some organisms have become extinct.
- Extinction may be caused by:
  - changes to the environment over geological (long periods of) time
  - new predators
  - new diseases
  - new, more successful competitors
  - a single catastrophic event, e.g. massive volcanic eruptions or collisions with asteroids.
- For example, the great auk is now extinct due to over-hunting.

Evolutionary Trees

- Evolutionary trees are a method used by scientists to show how they think organisms are related.
- They use current classification data for living organisms and fossil data for extinct organisms.

Great Auk

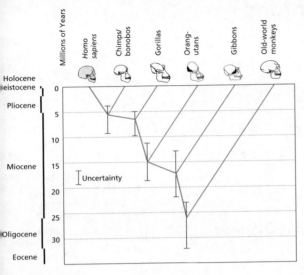

Speciation

- The lowest level in Linnaeus's classification system is the 'species'.
- Members of a species are similar enough to be able to breed with each other and produce fertile offspring.
- Alfred Russel Wallace, who proposed a theory for evolution, also worked on a theory of **speciation**, i.e. how new species develop:
  1. Populations become physically isolated from each other, e.g. by a mountain range or ocean.
  2. Genetic variation is present between the two populations.
  3. Natural selection operates differently in the two populations.
  4. The populations become so different that successful interbreeding is no longer possible.
- Wallace's theory is supported by recent studies.

> ### Key Point
>
> Darwin and Wallace both visited many islands before putting forward their theories. New species often form on islands, because they are isolated from populations on other islands.

Quick Test

1. What classification group comes between 'class' and 'family' in Linnaeus' system?
2. How many domains are there in the current classification system?
3. The binomial name for domestic cats is *Felis catus*. What does this tell you about how they are classified?
4. Give **two** reasons why a species may become extinct.
5. How can scientists tell if two groups or organisms have become different species?

> ### Key Words
>
> binomial system
> genus
> species
> three-domain system
> extinct
> speciation

Pathogens and Disease

1 **a)** Define the term 'vector'. [1]

b) What organism acts as a vector for the protist that causes malaria? [1]

c) Suggest **two** ways in which people can protect themselves from this vector. [2]

Total Marks _____ / 4

Human Defences Against Disease

1 **a)** Use words from the box to complete the sentences about vaccination.

Each word may be used once, more than once or not at all.

| antibodies | antibiotics | antiseptics | dead | live | red | toxins | white |

During vaccination, _____ or weakened pathogens are injected into the body.

This causes _____ blood cells to make _____.

Later, when _____ pathogens enter the body, they are destroyed quickly. [4]

b) Vaccinations can provide immunity.

Give **one** other way by which a person can become immune to a pathogen. [1]

2 In March 2009, a nine-year-old girl was found to be infected with a new strain of the H1N1 swine flu virus. Over the next year many more people were found to have the swine flu virus.

The graph in **Figure 1** shows the number of reported cases of swine flu in the first 10 days of May 2010.

a) How many cases of swine flu had been reported by 5th May? [1]

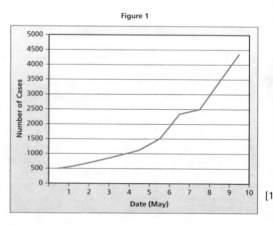

Figure 1

b) Which period showed the largest increase in the number of reported cases? [1]

c) Suggest why the spread of disease was so rapid. [2]

d) Why is it difficult to kill viruses inside the body? [2]

> Total Marks _____ / 11

Treating Diseases

1. Scientists often need to test bacteria for sensitivity to different antibiotics in order to decide the best antibiotic for treatment.
This is the method used:

1. Heat nutrient agar to 121°C.
2. Pour into a Petri dish and leave to cool.
3. Spread the bacteria onto nutrient agar in a Petri dish.
4. Place small filter-paper discs containing different antibiotics onto the agar.
5. Incubate the inoculated Petri dishes for 16 hours and then examine them.

a) What is nutrient agar? [2]

b) What is the main reason for heating the agar to 121°C? [1]
Tick **one** box.

So it pours easily ☐

To dissolve the nutrients ☐

To kill any microorganisms ☐

c) Why are the inoculated Petri dishes incubated before measurements are taken? [1]

d) **Figure 1** shows the Petri dish after incubation.
Erythromycin was found to be the most effective antibiotic.
Penicillin had no effect at all on the bacteria.

Figure 1

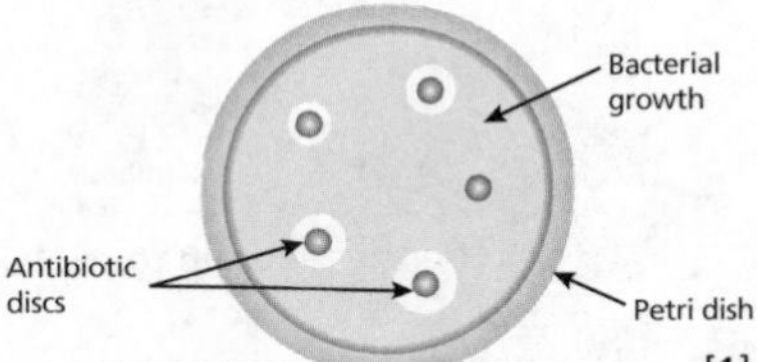

- Bacterial growth
- Antibiotic discs
- Petri dish

i) Label the antibiotic disc containing erythromycin with an **E**. [1]

ii) Label the antibiotic disc containing penicillin with a **P**. [1]

Review Questions

2   HT **Figure 2** shows the stages of making a monoclonal antibody.

Figure 2

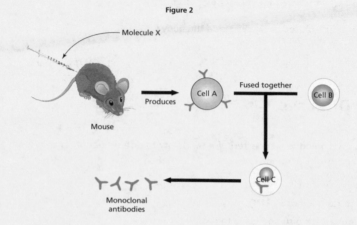

Molecule X

Mouse

Produces

Cell A

Fused together

Cell B

Cell C

Monoclonal antibodies

a) Identify the different types of cells labelled **A**, **B** and **C** in the diagram.   [3

b) What type of molecule is **X**?   [1
   Tick **one** box.

   Antibiotic ☐   Antigen ☐

   Antibody ☐   Antiseptic ☐

c) Monoclonal antibodies can be used to treat some types of cancer.
   This process is shown in **Figure 3**.

Figure 3

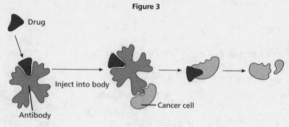

Drug

Inject into body

Antibody

Cancer cell

   Use the diagram to explain how this process works.   [4

3   Many people in the world have a disease called arthritis.
    Their joints become very painful.

    Here is an article about a new arthritis drug.

To Use or Not to Use?

Arthritis is a very painful condition.

The problem with many drugs used to treat arthritis is that they have side effects.

One new drug was recently developed and tested on animals like mice and rats with no side effects. However, after a long-term study on human patients, side effects were noticed.

In this study, the drug was compared with a placebo. After 18 months of taking the drug, the risk of a patient having a heart attack was 15 out of 1000 compared with 7.5 out of 1000 for patients taking the placebo.

A decision has to be made about whether to use the drug even though it increases the risk of heart disease.

a) It is important that all drugs are tested on humans, and not just animals, before they are widely used.

Why is this? [1]

b) The long-term study used a placebo.

What is a placebo and why is it used? [3]

c) Some new drugs for arthritis are still allowed to be used even though they carry a slight risk.

Why do you think that this is? [2]

Total Marks _____ / 20

Plant Disease

1. Vinay is growing tomato plants in his garden.
He notices that the leaves of the plant have patches that are much lighter in colour.
He thinks that his plants may be infected by tobacco mosaic virus (TMV).

a) The presence of very light green patches on the leaves may mean that the plants will not grow as well.

Explain why this is. [3]

b) Vinay's gardening book says that the green patches might be caused by a lack of magnesium ions in the soil.

Why could this have an effect on the leaves? [1]

c) HT What could Vinay do to find out for certain if his plants had tobacco mosaic virus? [1]

Total Marks _____ / 5

Practice Questions

Sexual and Asexual Reproduction

1 **a)** Use the words in the box to label the cell in **Figure 1**.

> chromosomes   nucleus   cytoplasm   cell membrane

Figure 1

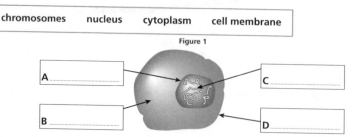

A ....

B ....

C ....

D ....

[4]

b) Choose the correct word to complete each sentence.

Sexual reproduction is the **division / separation / fusion** of the male and female gametes.

The resulting offspring will contain **DNA / cells / enzymes** from both parents.

This gives rise to **fertilisation / differentiation / variation.**

[3]

2 **Figure 2** shows the sequence of events used to clone sheep by embryo transplantation.

Figure 2

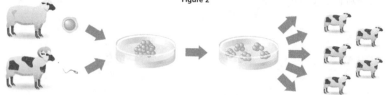

a) Use words from the box to complete the sentences.

> gametes   old   implanted   shocked   directed   characteristics
> sexual   wombs   asexual   sterile   stomachs   specialised

A male and female sheep with the desired .... are mated using IVF.

This is an example of .... reproduction.

Before the cells become ...., the embryo is split into several clumps.

These are then .... into the .... of surrogate sheep. All the resulting offspring are identical to each other.

[5]

b) Why would farmers want to use embryo transplants rather than more natural methods of reproduction? [2]

c) Explain why the offspring from the above process will be identical to each other but not identical to the original male and female sheep. [4]

d) Scientists now have the technology to clone human embryos.

Give **one** medical reason why cloning human embryos might be permitted. [1]

Total Marks _____ / 19

DNA and Protein Synthesis

1 The genetic material in the nucleus of a cell is made from DNA.

a) In which structures is the DNA contained? [1]

b) In terms of DNA, describe what a gene is and what it does. [3]

c) What is the name given to the shape of a DNA molecule? [1]

d) HT In terms of DNA, what is a mutation? [1]

Total Marks _____ / 6

Patterns of Inheritance

1 **a)** Circle the correct pairs of human sex chromosomes.

| XY and YY | XX and XY | XX and YY | XF and XM |

[1]

b) In the space to the right,
draw a genetic cross diagram
to show how these chromosomes
are involved in sex inheritance. [2]

2 Draw **one** line from each definition to the correct genetic term.

Definition	Term
both alleles are the same	phenotype
two different alleles	heterozygous
what the organism looks like	homozygous
an allele that is always expressed if present	dominant

[3]

3 Fruit flies are often used in genetic crosses.

There are two types of wings on fruit flies: short or normal.

Answer the following questions.

Use the letter **N** to represent normal wings and **n** to represent short wings.

a) What is the phenotype for a fly that has the homozygous dominant genotype? [1]

b) A heterozygous male fly mates with a homozygous recessive female.

Complete the diagram in **Figure 2** for this genetic cross.

c) What will be the ratio of normal wings to short wings in the offspring?

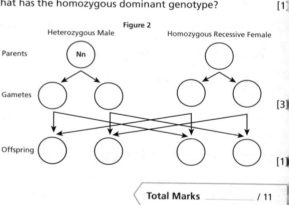

Figure 2

Heterozygous Male

Homozygous Recessive Female

Parents

Nn

Gametes

[3]

Offspring

[1]

Total Marks _____ / 11

Variation and Evolution

1 It is thought that many years ago members of the giraffe family had short necks.

Giraffes now have longer necks, which allow them to reach food higher in the trees.

a) Use Charles Darwin's theory of natural selection to explain how modern giraffes with longer necks may have evolved. [3]

b) Lamarck was another scientist with ideas about evolution.

He had a theory that some giraffes grew longer necks in order to reach the leaves high on the trees.

These giraffes were then more successful and were able to breed and pass their long necks onto their offspring.

Explain why Lamarck's theory is **not** correct. [2]

c) Darwin also suggested that humans and apes evolved from a common ancestor.

Give **two** reasons why Darwin's theories were not accepted by some people. [2]

Total Marks _____ / 7

Manipulating Genes

1 HT **Figure 1** shows the **first** stage in the process of insulin production using genetic engineering.

Figure 1

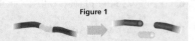

a) What do scientists use to 'cut out' the insulin gene from the chromosome? [1]

b) The 'cut' gene is then inserted into a bacterium.

Why are bacteria good host cells for the 'cut' insulin gene? [2]

Total Marks _____ / 3

Classification

1 a) Describe **one** way in which fossils are formed. [1]

b) Explain why fossils can be quite hard to find. [1]

c) Many fossils are of animals that are extinct.

Give **three** factors that could contribute to the extinction of a species. [3]

d) Give an example of a **species** that is now extinct. [1]

Total Marks _____ / 6

Sexual and Asexual Reproduction

1 Spider plants reproduce asexually by producing structures called stolons.

This is shown in **Figure 1**.

Circle the correct word to complete each sentence.

Figure 1

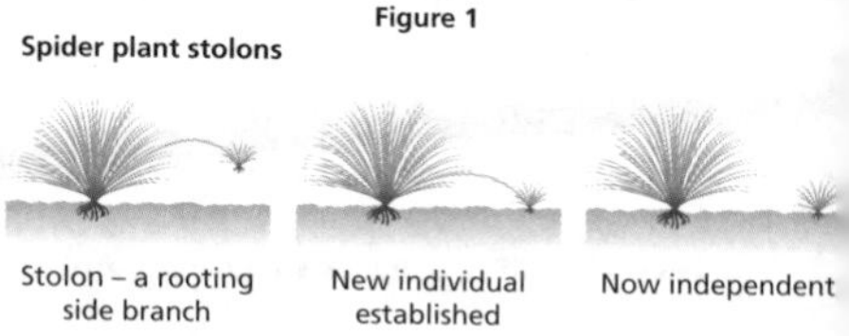

Spider plant stolons

Stolon – a rooting side branch   New individual established   Now independent

a) Asexual reproduction needs **one / two** spider plant(s).   [1

b) Asexual reproduction does not involve the production of **gametes / DNA**.   [1

c) The genes in the new spider plants will be **the same as / different to** the parent genes.   [1

d) The new spider plant is called a **shoot / clone**.   [1

2 Mitosis is the division of body cells to make new cells.

a) When is mitosis **not** used for cell division?
Tick **one** box.

Asexual reproduction ☐

Gamete production ☐

Repair ☐

Growth ☐   [1]

b) Complete the sentences about mitosis.

A copy of each _____ is made before a cell divides.

The new cell has the same _____ information as the _____ cell.

Meiosis takes place in the testes, and produces sperm containing 23 _____.   [4]

c) What type of cell is produced in meiosis?   [1]

3 The statements below describe the different stages in adult cell cloning.
They are in the wrong order.

a) Number the statements **1** to **6** to show the correct order.
Two have been done for you.

The nucleus is removed from an egg cell and discarded. ☐

The embryo is implanted in the womb of another cow. ☐

The nucleus of the body cell is placed into the empty egg cell. ☐

A body cell is taken from a prize bull. ☐

The cell is zapped with electricity and starts to divide to form an embryo. 5

An unfertilised egg cell is taken from a cow. 2 [3]

b) At stage 5, how are the cells prompted to divide? [1]

Total Marks _____ / 14

DNA and Protein Synthesis

1 HT Explain how genes control protein synthesis. [4]

2 a) Define the term 'genome'. [1]

b) Suggest **two** important uses of this data about the human genome. [2]

Total Marks _____ / 7

Patterns of Inheritance

1 History tells how King Henry VIII was so desperate to have a male heir that he divorced or disposed of all his wives who were unable to produce a son.

a) What sex chromosomes are found in eggs? [1]

b) What sex chromosomes are found in sperm? [1]

c) Use your answers to part **a)** and **b)** to explain why it was unfair of Henry to blame his wives for the lack of a son. [2]

2 Rita likes to grow plants.

One particular plant she grows can either have red flowers or white flowers.

She decides to cross a red flowered plant with a white flowered plant.

a) Complete the table below to show this genetic cross.

Use **R** to represent the dominant allele and **r** to represent the recessive allele. [4]

		White Flower (rr)	
		Genotype of Ovum (r)	Genotype of Ovum (r)
Red Flower (Rr)	Genotype of Pollen (R)		
	Genotype of Pollen (r)		

b) Rita grows 24 plants using the seeds from this cross.

Predict the number of red flowered and white flowered plants that are produced. [2]

c) Why is it unlikely that the actual numbers of each type of plant will exactly match this prediction? [2]

Total Marks _____ / 12

Variation and Evolution

1 Variation can be due to inherited factors, environmental factors or a combination of both.

Cathy and Drew are sister and brother.

Table 1 shows how they are different.

Table 1

Cathy	Drew	Inherited (I), Environmental (E) or Both (B)
tongue roller	non roller	
not colour blind	colour blind	
1.5m tall	1.6m tall	
speaks French	does not speak French	

Complete **Table 1** to show if each difference is caused by inherited factors **(I)**, environmental factors **(E)** or a combination of both **(B)**. [4]

Total Marks _____ / 4

Manipulating Genes

1 Farmers have been using selective breeding for thousands of years to produce crops and animals with desirable characteristics.

a) Suggest **two** characteristics that might be desirable in food crops. [2]

b) Suggest two characteristics that might be desirable in dairy cows. [2]

c) Describe the main stages in the process of selective breeding. [4]

d) Developments in biotechnology mean that genes can now be inserted into crop plants to give them desirable characteristics.

What is the term used to describe crops that have had their genes altered in this way? [1]

Total Marks _____ / 9

Classification

1 Scientists frequently study the distribution of the snail, *Cepaea nemoralis*. The snail has a shell that can be brown or yellow.

a) i) What genus does the snail belong to? [1]

ii) How could scientists prove that the different coloured snails were all the same species? [2]

b) Scientists believe that shell colour affects the body temperature of the snails. Snails with dark shells warm up faster than those with light shells. In cold areas, this would be advantageous to the dark-coloured snail.

The average annual temperature in Scotland is 2°C lower than in England.

Use the theory of natural selection to explain why populations of the snail in Scotland contain a higher percentage of dark-coloured snails? [3]

c) Explain how two new species of snails could be formed from two different populations of *Cepaea*. [4]

Total Marks _____ / 10

Answers

Page 5 Quick Test
1. Use of a handkerchief / tissue
2. So that microorganisms from the uncooked meat do not contaminate the cooked meat
3. It is not a barrier method of contraception
4. To prevent the fungal spores spreading to healthy leaves

Page 7 Quick Test
1. With acid
2. The process that a white blood cell uses to engulf pathogens
3. Antibodies
4. To stimulate antibody production without making the person too ill

Page 9 Quick Test
1. Antibiotics only kill bacteria (HIV is caused by a virus)
2. Resistant
3. Because willow bark contains aspirin
4. Neither the patient nor the doctor know which medication the patient is taking

Page 11 Quick Test
1. It reduces chlorophyll content so less light is trapped
2. Liquid (containing sugars) from the phloem
3. Nitrates are needed to make proteins

Page 12 Pathogens and Disease
1. Four correctly drawn lines [3] (2 marks for two correct lines and 1 mark for one correct line)
bacterium – salmonella
virus – measles
protist – malaria
fungus – rose black spot

Page 12 Human Defences Against Disease
1. dead [1]; weakened [1]; antibodies [1]; immune [1] (first two marks can be given in any order)

> Do not use the term 'resistant' here. Resistance is when an organism is born with the ability not to get a disease.

2. a) Fever [1]; red skin rash [1]
   b) It can be fatal [1]
   c) i) 84% [1]
      ii) 1998 [1]; 2003 [1]
      iii) Concern over side effects of the vaccine [1]
3. a) Stops insects biting [1]; so they do not pass on pathogens / diseases [1]; such as malaria [1]
   b) Vaccinations prevent a person from

getting a disease [1]; the antibodies need to be in the blood when the pathogen is contracted [1]; otherwise the pathogen may cause illness before antibodies are made [1]
4. Jim [1]; Bill [1]

Page 14 Treating Diseases
1. a) $\frac{(5+5+6+7)}{4}$ [1]; = 5.8 [1]
   b) Plate 4 / bathroom cleaner [1]
   c) To act as a control [1]
   d) She has repeated them four times and calculated the mean [1]
2. a) i) A chemical made by microorganisms [1]; that kills bacteria / stops bacteria reproducing [1]
      ii) Viruses [1]
   b) i) MRSA [1]
      ii) Antibiotics are only available by prescription [1]; only prescribed when necessary [1]; patients are told that they must finish the dose [1]
3. a) 5, 3, 1, 4, 2 [3] (1 mark for one correct; 2 marks for two correct)
   b) To see if they work [1]; to see if they are harmful / have side effects [1]
   c) i) A tablet / liquid that does not contain the drug [1]
      ii) To compare with the effect the drug is having / as a control [1]; to make sure the drug is not just producing a psychological effect [1]

Page 15 Plant Disease
1. a) Phloem [1]
   b) They take food from the phloem [1]; so less is available to the plant for growth / making new cells [1]
   c) The aphids may take up pathogens from the phloem when feeding [1]; and pass them on, via their mouthparts, when they feed on another plant [1]
   d) Tobacco plants contain poisons [1]; which may kill insect pests [1]

Page 17 Quick Test
1. Long shoots that are produced in asexual reproduction
2. Four
3. 39
4. Sexual reproduction

Page 19 Quick Test
1. DNA
2. A gene
3. Sugar, phosphate and a base
4. A random change in the DNA
5. To switch genes on or off

Page 21 Quick Test
1. Alleles
2. Heterozygous
3. Recessive
4. X and Y

Page 23 Quick Test
1. Darwin (and Wallace)
2. Any one of: there was not enough direct evidence; the mechanism for inheritance was not known; it went against the church
3. Lamarck
4. Any one of: soft-bodied organisms did not fossilise; fossils have been destroyed

Page 25 Quick Test
1. Any one of: high milk yield; fat content of milk; high-quality beef (any other sensible answer)
2. An enzyme
3. Worries about the effects on wild plant populations / human health
4. To stimulate the egg to divide

Page 27 Quick Test
1. Order
2. Three
3. Its genus is *Felis* and species is *(Felis) catus*
4. Any two of: changes to the environment over long periods of time; new predators; new diseases; more successful competitors; a single catastrophic event
5. They can no longer mate to produce fertile offspring

Page 28 Pathogens and Disease
1. a) An organism that carries a disease from one host to another without being infected itself [1]
   b) Mosquito [1]
   c) Insect repellent / killing the mosquitoes [1]; mosquito nets [1]

Page 28 Human Defences Against Disease
1. a) dead [1]; white [1]; antibodies [1]; live [1]
   b) By becoming infected with the disease [1]
2. a) 1250 [1]
   b) 8th to 10th May [1]
   c) People were not immune [1]; they had not been vaccinated / no vaccine was available [1]
   d) Viruses are inside cells for much of the time [1]; so drugs / antibodies find it more difficult to reach them [1]

Page 29 Treating Diseases
1. a) A type of jelly [1]; containing chemicals / nutrients that bacteria need to grow [1]

b) To kill any microorganisms **[1]**
c) To give the bacteria time to grow / be killed **[1]**
d) i) Disc with the widest clear area labelled, E **[1]**
   ii) Disc with no clear area labelled, P. **[1]**
a) A = white blood cell / lymphocyte **[1]**; B = tumour cell **[1]**; C = hybridoma cell **[1]**
b) Antigen **[1]**
c) The drug attaches to the antibody **[1]**; the antibody attaches itself to a cancer cell **[1]**; the drug enters the cancer cell **[1]**; and the cancer cell is destroyed **[1]**
a) Because the drug may work differently on humans compared with other animals. **[1]**
b) A placebo is a tablet / liquid containing no drug **[1]**; used for comparison (control) **[1]**; to make sure any positive responses are not just a psychological response to taking a pill / medicine **[1]**
c) Need to balance the risk with the benefit gained **[1]**; a slight risk of side effects may be acceptable if the benefit is that it relieves great pain **[1]**

age 31 Plant Disease
a) There is less chlorophyll present **[1]**; so less photosynthesis takes place **[1]**; and less food / glucose is made **[1]**
b) Magnesium ions are needed to make chlorophyll **[1]**
c) Take infected plant to a laboratory / use a testing kit **[1]**

age 32 Sexual and Asexual eproduction
a) A = nucleus **[1]**; B = cytoplasm **[1]**; C = chromosomes **[1]**; D = cell membrane **[1]**
b) fusion **[1]**; DNA **[1]**; variation **[1]**
a) characteristics **[1]**; sexual **[1]**; specialised **[1]**; implanted **[1]**; wombs **[1]**
b) Many more offspring can be produced **[1]**; all the offspring will be identical to each other with the desired characteristics **[1]**
c) The offspring are identical because they all come from the same zygote **[1]**; therefore, they have the same genetic information **[1]**; they have some genetic information from the father **[1]**; and some from the mother as the original embryo was created using sexual reproduction (sperm and egg) **[1]**
d) To obtain stem cells for treating diseases / damaged cells **[1]**

age 33 DNA and Protein Synthesis
a) Chromosomes **[1]**
b) A section of DNA **[1]**; that codes for

a particular sequence of amino acids **[1]**; to make a specific protein **[1]**
c) Double helix **[1]**
d) A spontaneous change in the structure of the DNA **[1]**

Page 33 Patterns of Inheritance
1. a) XX and XY **[1]**
   b)
   (1 mark for each correct row **[2]**)
2. Four correctly drawn lines **[3]** (2 marks for two correct lines and 1 mark for one correct line)
   both alleles are the same – homozygous
   two different alleles – heterozygous
   what the organism looks like – phenotype
   an allele that is always expressed if present – dominant
3. a) NN **[1]**
   b) Correct parent: nn **[1]**; correct gametes: N, n, n, n **[1]**; correct offspring: Nn, nn, Nn, nn **[1]**
   c) 1 : 1 **[1]**

Page 34 Variation and Evolution
1. a) The giraffes showed variation **[1]**; longer-necked individuals were more likely to survive as they could get more food **[1]**; they breed and pass on the gene / characteristic to their offspring **[1]**
   b) Changes that happen during an individual's lifetime are not passed on **[1]**; because they do not change the genetic material **[1]**
   c) **Any two of:** There was a lack of direct evidence at the time **[1]**; the mechanism for inheritance was not known **[1]**; people were very religious at the time and didn't like that it contradicted the creation story **[1]**

Page 35 Manipulating Genes
1. a) Enzymes **[1]**
   b) **Any two of:** they easily take up genes in plasmids **[1]**; they use them to make proteins **[1]**; they replicate rapidly **[1]**

Page 35 Classification
1. a) **Any one of:** dead organisms are coved in mud and compressed **[1]**; from hard parts of animals that do not decay **[1]**; from parts of organisms that have not decayed because the conditions prevented it **[1]**; when parts of an organism are replaced by other materials as they decay **[1]**; preserved traces of organisms, e.g. footprints **[1]**
   b) May be deep in rock / not many to find as they have been destroyed **[1]**

c) **Any three of:** geographical changes **[1]**; new predators **[1]**; new diseases **[1]**; more competitors **[1]**; catastrophic events **[1]**; human actions **[1]**
d) Great auk / dodo **[1]** (Accept any other sensible answer)

Page 36 Sexual and Asexual Reproduction
1. a) one **[1]**
   b) gametes **[1]**
   c) the same as **[1]**
   d) clone **[1]**
2. a) Gamete production **[1]**
   b) chromosome **[1]**; genetic **[1]**; parent / old / original **[1]**; chromosomes **[1]**
   c) Gametes **[1]**
3. a) 3, 6, 4, 1 **[3]** (2 marks for 2 correct; 1 mark for 1 correct)
   b) By giving them an electric shock **[1]**

Page 37 DNA and Protein Synthesis
1. A gene is a length of DNA **[1]**; DNA is made up of a sequence of bases **[1]**; the order of bases codes for the order of amino acids in a protein **[1]**; three bases for each amino acid **[1]**
2. a) All the genetic material within an organism **[1]**
   b) **Any two of:** doctors can search for genes linked to different types of disorder **[1]**; it can help scientists to understand the cause of inherited disorders and how to treat them **[1]** (Accept any other sensible answer)

Page 37 Patterns of Inheritance
1. a) X **[1]**
   b) X or Y **[1]**
   c) A boy is produced when a Y sperm from the father fertilises an egg **[1]**; all the eggs contain X chromosomes **[1]**

   Make sure you only put one sex chromosome in a sex cell, they can only be X or Y not XX or XY.

2. a)

		White Flower (rr)	
		Genotype of Ovum (r)	Genotype of Ovum (r)
Red Flower (Rr)	Genotype of Pollen (R)	Rr **[1]**	Rr **[1]**
	Genotype of Pollen (r)	rr **[1]**	rr **[1]**

Answers

b) 12 red **[1]**; 12 white **[1]**
c) This is only a probability **[1]**; fusion of gametes is random / only gets close to 1 : 1 with large numbers **[1]**

Page 38 Variation and Evolution
1. Top to bottom: I **[1]**; I **[1]**; B **[1]**; E **[1]**

Page 39 Manipulating Genes
1. **a)** A high yield **[1]**; resistance to disease **[1]** (Accept any other sensible answer)
   b) A high milk yield **[1]**; fat content of milk **[1]** (Accept any other sensible answer)
   c) Choose parents that show the desired characteristic **[1]**; breed them together **[1]**; select offspring with the desired characteristic and breed **[1]**; continue over many generations **[1]**
   d) Genetically modified / GM   **[1]**

Page 39 Classification
1. **a) i)** *Cepaea*   **[1]**
      ii) Mate them together **[1]**; see if they produced fertile offspring **[1]**
   b) Dark-shelled snails are better adapted to cold conditions **[1]**; so they are more likely to survive and breed **[1]**; and pass on the dark characteristic to the offspring **[1]**
   c) Speciation **[1]**; the populations become isolated so cannot reproduce with each other **[1]**; natural selection happens differently in the two populations / areas **[1]**; they become so different they can no longer breed to produce fertile offspring **[1]**

Notes

Notes